THE LONG MARCH

A Famine Gift for Ireland

WRITTEN AND ILLUSTRATED BY

Marie-Louise Fitzpatrick

CHOCTAW EDITING AND FOREWORD BY

Gary WhiteDeer

For my family, with love, and to your memory, Dad

WOLFHOUND PRESS

Foreword

In 1847, an impoverished group of Choctaw Indians in America collected from their meagre resources the sum of $170 to send toward relief of the Irish Potato Famine. In today's money that donation would be worth more than $5,000.

This is the historical essence of *The Long March*, a recounting of how a poor, dispossessed people reached out across an ocean to help another. It is a universal story, one that belongs to each of us.

Marie-Louise Fitzpatrick has taken a remarkable history and given it the breath of life. In preparing for its retelling, the author/illustrator journeyed from Ireland to Oklahoma to research with the Choctaw elders, state historians, ethnologists, and tribal tradition bearers. The result is a stunning portrait of 1847 Choctaw daily arts and lifeways.

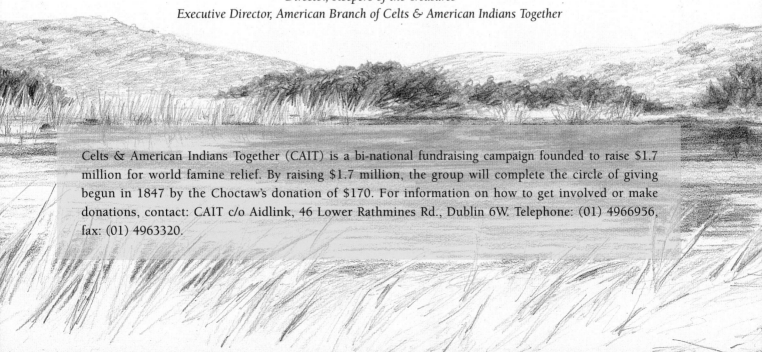

Period ornaments, clothing, and excerpts from Choctaw daily life have been accurately etched in beautiful detail and imagery, and now shine like recovered tribal heirlooms. Story characters were sketched just as accurately. My son Quanah and my aunt Lena Noah served as models for the boy Choona and his great-grandmother.

More than this, *The Long March* is cast within the universal time dilemma of a boy struggling to become an adult. Choona faces questions that each of us must answer: What can we do, what should we do, about repression and world suffering? Fortunately for Choona, ancient tribal values help him to resolve these age-old human questions.

Just as importantly, these age-old questions allow Native Americans to be introduced to young readers as people rather than as colourful stereotypes. Issues of social justice touch all of our lives. How each society chooses to respond to them, perhaps more than technological and material progress, determines to what extent any society may be called civilised.

The Long March is a graceful, moving account of an episode in human history that is also a parable for our time. Like a parable, this book is of timeless truth and beauty.

Gary WhiteDeer
Oklahoma Choctaw
Director, Keepers of the Treasures
Executive Director, American Branch of Celts & American Indians Together

Celts & American Indians Together (CAIT) is a bi-national fundraising campaign founded to raise $1.7 million for world famine relief. By raising $1.7 million, the group will complete the circle of giving begun in 1847 by the Choctaw's donation of $170. For information on how to get involved or make donations, contact: CAIT c/o Aidlink, 46 Lower Rathmines Rd., Dublin 6W. Telephone: (01) 4966956, fax: (01) 4963320.

I am an old man now. They call me Tom, the name the missionaries gave me. Back then I was still known by my Choctaw name, Choona, the Skinny One. It is hard to remember being a child. It is all just fragments and blurred faces, a smell, a room, a toy, a favourite tree, but I remember that year so clearly. It was 1847. I was fourteen years old. When they called me a boy, I was insulted, and when they said I was nearly a man, I was confused.

I was in the yard playing with the ballsticks when Father and my uncle, Moshi, arrived home from Skullyville. The little pack horses were laden with trade goods. Mother, Great-Grandmother, and my two sisters were soon pulling the parcels open and exclaiming over the bolts of bright cloth Father had bought, the new cooking pot, some silver combs, and glass beads. I admired a new axe and listened as Father and Moshi related the latest news from around the Choctaw Nation. The story they seemed most interested in was of a great famine, far away, in a country called Ireland. The district chiefs had decided that the whole tribe should hear about it. Riders had been sent to call the people to Skullyville the following evening.

"I don't understand," said Mother. "What has this story to do with us?"

Moshi looked at his sister.

"This story is our story," he said.

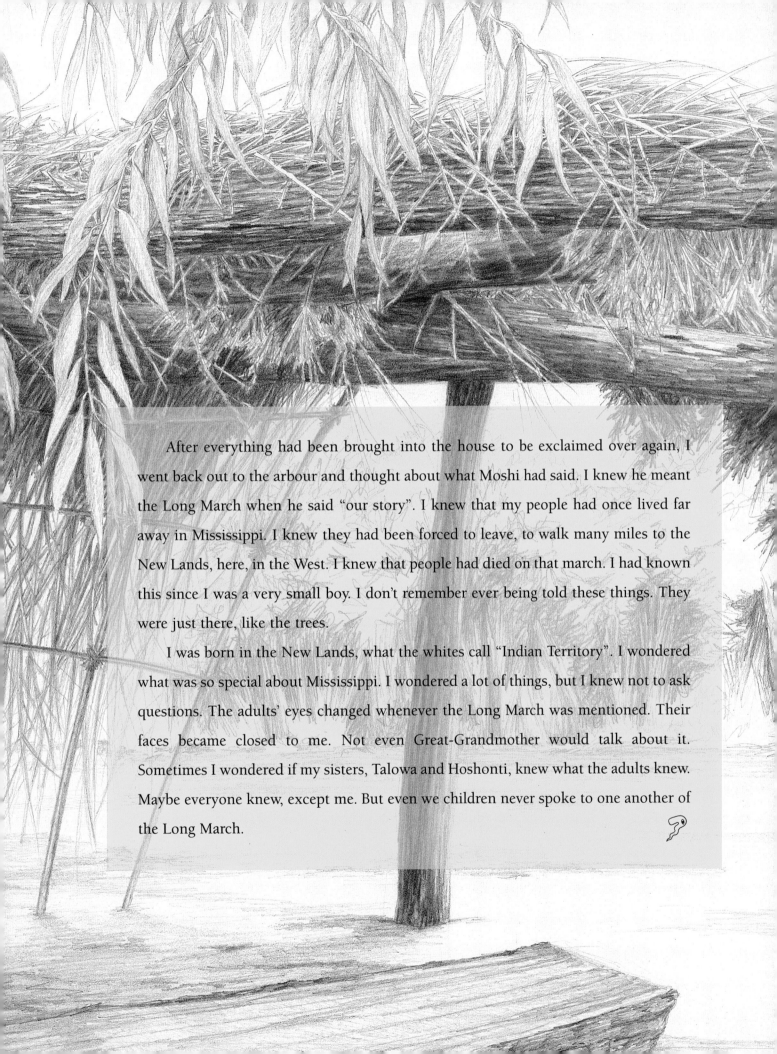

After everything had been brought into the house to be exclaimed over again, I went back out to the arbour and thought about what Moshi had said. I knew he meant the Long March when he said "our story". I knew that my people had once lived far away in Mississippi. I knew they had been forced to leave, to walk many miles to the New Lands, here, in the West. I knew that people had died on that march. I had known this since I was a very small boy. I don't remember ever being told these things. They were just there, like the trees.

I was born in the New Lands, what the whites call "Indian Territory". I wondered what was so special about Mississippi. I wondered a lot of things, but I knew not to ask questions. The adults' eyes changed whenever the Long March was mentioned. Their faces became closed to me. Not even Great-Grandmother would talk about it. Sometimes I wondered if my sisters, Talowa and Hoshonti, knew what the adults knew. Maybe everyone knew, except me. But even we children never spoke to one another of the Long March.

We travelled to Skullyville the following evening to join my mother's clan for the meeting that had been called. My father was of the Okla Hannalei, the Six Towns Clan of the tribe, but our family belonged to the Ahithabo Apat Okla, the Potato Eating People. The adults gathered outside the agency meeting house. Great-Grandmother and Mother went to sit with the other women. My sisters joined the other children to play in the shadows beyond the adult circle. I hovered at its edges unsure and, I hoped, unseen.

Talowa, Hoshonti, and I were proud to have a great-grandmother. Few of our friends even had grandparents. Great-Grandmother was the oldest person in our tribe. She was called Talihoyo, Rockwoman. When she was young an enemy tribe's warriors had sneaked across the river into the cornfields where she and the other women were working. Instead of screaming and running away, she encouraged the women to stand their ground and throw rocks at the warriors until they turned and fled back across the river. Great-Grandmother was much respected and everyone greeted her as she sat down.

Soon the circle was packed and noisy. Moshi stepped forward and asked for quiet. My uncle was the Minkoapilachi, the ceremonial speaker for the tribal leaders. He gave the formal welcome to bring the people together in council. Then he began to tell the tribe the story he and Father had heard the day before.

He spoke of a country far away where the people ate potatoes. Now the potatoes were rotting in the ground. There was nothing else to eat and the people were sick and starving. Whole villages of people were leaving their homes and walking the land in search of food. They were eating the leaves from the trees and the grass from the ground in a desperate attempt to stay alive. They were dying as they walked. The mouths of the dead were stained green.

Moshi said the Memphis Committee had brought the story to the tribal leaders from Washington, D.C., where a big meeting had been held to see what could be done to help these Irish people.

"We too are being asked to help them," said Moshi.

Moshi waited to see what people would say to this, but no one spoke.

"We are being asked to help them," repeated Moshi.

Still there was silence, and then a man called Mishima Abi spoke. He was a respected warrior and had taken enemy lives in battle. He spoke forcefully.

"These people are Nahullo, Europeans," he said.

"The Nahullo have come to our
land and taken it from us. They have
caused our people to die. It is because of
them that the bones of our people lie scat-
tered along the trail of the Long March. The
Nahullo only take, they do not give. Why
should we help them?"

Some people murmured in agreement.

Mishima Abi lifted his hands in appeal.

"Why should we help the Nahullo? Why?
Why?"

Tension filled the circle.

The war words had been effective.

The silence stretched out.

Then Great-Grandmother cleared her throat to
speak. Immediately everyone turned to hear what Talihoyo
would say. She had the attention of the whole council. Even the children
crept forward from the shadows. Her words would carry weight. She was our
oldest elder.

"Long ago," she began, "when the world was young, the ground split open and
the Choctaw people walked out of the earth into the living land..."

I thought my great-grandmother had gotten off the point, but I didn't care. I loved
her stories. I slid down to the floor beside my sisters.

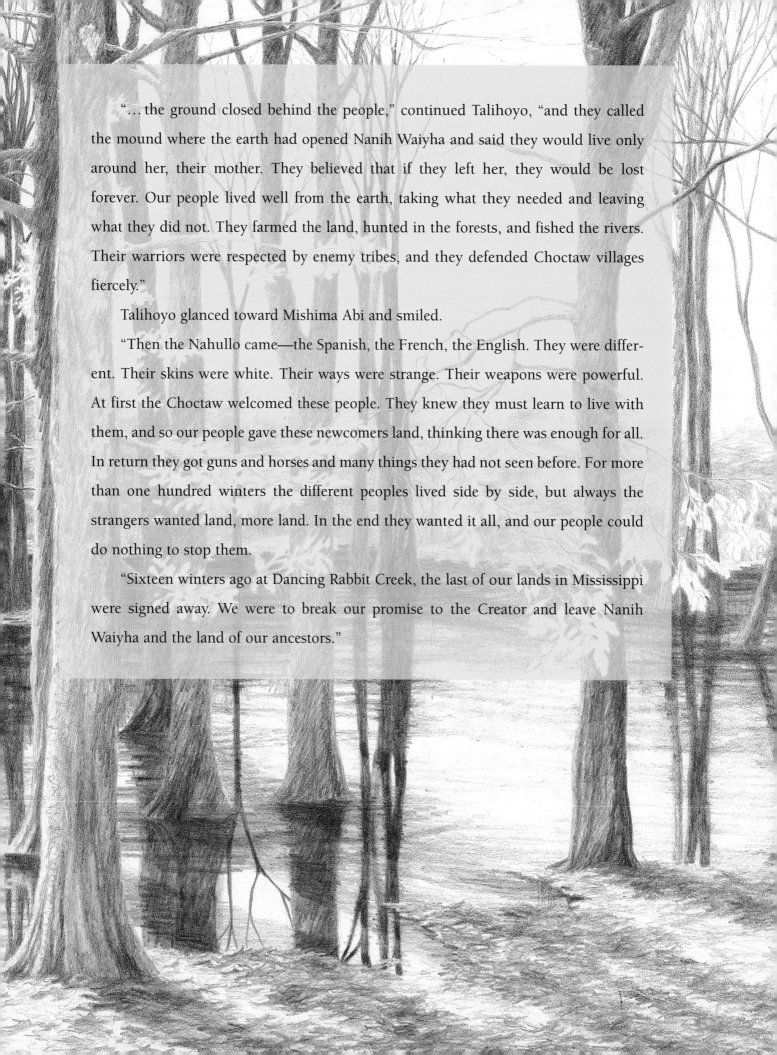

"...the ground closed behind the people," continued Talihoyo, "and they called the mound where the earth had opened Nanih Waiyha and said they would live only around her, their mother. They believed that if they left her, they would be lost forever. Our people lived well from the earth, taking what they needed and leaving what they did not. They farmed the land, hunted in the forests, and fished the rivers. Their warriors were respected by enemy tribes, and they defended Choctaw villages fiercely."

Talihoyo glanced toward Mishima Abi and smiled.

"Then the Nahullo came—the Spanish, the French, the English. They were different. Their skins were white. Their ways were strange. Their weapons were powerful. At first the Choctaw welcomed these people. They knew they must learn to live with them, and so our people gave these newcomers land, thinking there was enough for all. In return they got guns and horses and many things they had not seen before. For more than one hundred winters the different peoples lived side by side, but always the strangers wanted land, more land. In the end they wanted it all, and our people could do nothing to stop them.

"Sixteen winters ago at Dancing Rabbit Creek, the last of our lands in Mississippi were signed away. We were to break our promise to the Creator and leave Nanih Waiyha and the land of our ancestors."

Talihoyo was silent for a moment. I glanced around the circle. Everyone was quiet. I thought I saw dread in many eyes.

"We packed our belongings, those we could carry," said the old woman, "and we prepared to leave our homeland. We left behind our villages, our great fields of corn, our hunting grounds, the ancient burial places of our people. As we left, we kissed the ground and hugged the trees. The women clung to the bushes that overhung the Mississippi River.

"It was winter when the march began, thousands of us stretching to the horizon like a great herd of buffalo. It was cold. The rivers were freezing, the walking was hard. Soon the food was running out. The soldiers who marched us west to the New Lands could not explain why the blankets and food the government promised did not come.

"Every night we lay down to sleep on frozen ground, and every morning there were those who did not wake. People began to starve. Children became sick. The fever came and old and young slipped away from us into the spirit world. The ground became too hard to dig, and we could not bury our dead. We stripped their bodies and, as our ancestors once did, lifted them into the forks of the trees. In this way we buried them in the sky.

"The march went on, day after day, five hundred miles of swamp, river, forest, mountain, snow, ice. Five hundred miles of death. Now we walked alone, though together, each of us trying to stay alive. Trying to finish the day's journey. Waking each morning to walk again. Thousands of us walking in silence. Families fell behind to nurse the dying, to wait and watch with them, to leave their bodies behind, then to join the long march again—on and on, walking bones.

"Mountain Fork was the last river to cross. Our journey was over, they told us. Half our people were gone—

All the old ones.

All the small children.

Gone.

"Our journey was over, they told us. Yet we have walked in circles ever since. We have plowed new fields, but the land is foreign to us. We have built new homes, yet we are lost, just as our ancestors said we would be.

"I am old, without teeth," said Talihoyo. "I am half-blind, but when I close my eyes the faces of the dead come to me through the blackness. We have walked the trail of tears. The Irish people walk it now. We can help them as we could not help ourselves. Our help will be like an arrow shot through time. It will land many winters from now to wait as a blessing for our unborn generations."

Talihoyo was silent then. No one spoke, and I could see that the men and women were far away. I looked at my mother. Her gaze seemed to go right through me, as if I wasn't there. I dropped my eyes. After a while my father stood up. He addressed the council.

"We have only a little, but let us gather what we have and send it to Ireland."

The journey home was a quiet one. My sisters and I did not dare to break the silence.

I slept badly that night. I woke up angry. I had learned so much about my people's past, but still questions buzzed around in my brain like the flies that followed the Nahullo cattle. After breakfast, Father and Moshi took coins out of their handkerchiefs.

"So," said Father, "this money will go to the fund for the Irish Famine."

My mother and great-grandmother nodded their heads.

"No!" I suddenly heard myself shout. My family turned and looked at me in surprise.

"I … I don't know if I agree," I said, staring at the floor.

Mother and Father looked at one another.

"Mmm," said Moshi. "Well, perhaps you should go and think it over and let us know what you decide."

I went out to the arbour and sat down. I was shaking. I had never raised my voice to my father before. I didn't know why I had done it. I sat there, kicking the earth with my toe. After a while I heard the cabin door creak, and Great-Grandmother lowered herself onto the seat beside me.

"You are angry with us, Choona," she said.

"No, Hapokani."

"Mmm," she said, looking at my foot as I dug it into the earth. "It must be the ground you are angry with then."

I stopped my foot.

Great-Grandmother looked at the sky.

Silence.

Suddenly the words burst from me in a great rush.

"Why? Why did we let them drive us out? Why didn't we stay? Why didn't we fight? Why didn't my father fight?"

The old woman sighed.

"We asked ourselves all those questions then, but we knew we could not fight and win. There were those who stayed, even though their villages were burned and their lands taken. They must now struggle hard to survive. But if we had all tried to remain, we would have been forced out at gunpoint like the Cherokees, or dragged in chains like the Creek.

"Never think we chose the easy way. We chose to be free rather than to live as strangers in our own land. The Long March has never ended. We walk in two worlds every day. The mistake we have made has been in keeping our pain to ourselves, telling you children only what we had to.

The Long March is part of us all.

It is your story too."

"You had an older brother, Choona," Talihoyo said suddenly. "He had only seen one summer when he died out there on the trail. He was too young even to be given his Choctaw name."

She left me then and went back into the house.

I stood up and paced the yard. I had had a brother. Someone to run with. Someone to hunt and fight with. I could feel the space left by his death. It changed everything—the past, the future. The yard seemed to spin.

Brother, I never knew you, but I feel my loss.

The yard settled. The sky was still blue.

Now I understood—

My mother's eyes the night before, when Talihoyo made her walk the trail again.

The times I had come upon my father staring at the mountains and had known it was not these mountains that he saw.

I went back into the house.

Everyone looked up.

"Well?" Moshi asked.

"I think we should send the money to these people who walk as our people have walked," I said. I met my father's eyes and he smiled at me. Moshi took the coins from the table and put them in his buckskin pouch. He was to help gather and count the money the tribe donated. He went out to saddle his horse and I followed him.

"Do you think there will be much money to send, Moshi?" I asked.

"As much as people have to give," said my uncle.

"And will it do any good?" I asked.

"Yes, Choona," he said, smiling. "It already has. It has made our people face our past.

It has made us feel less helpless.

And it has made a certain boy learn to think like a man."

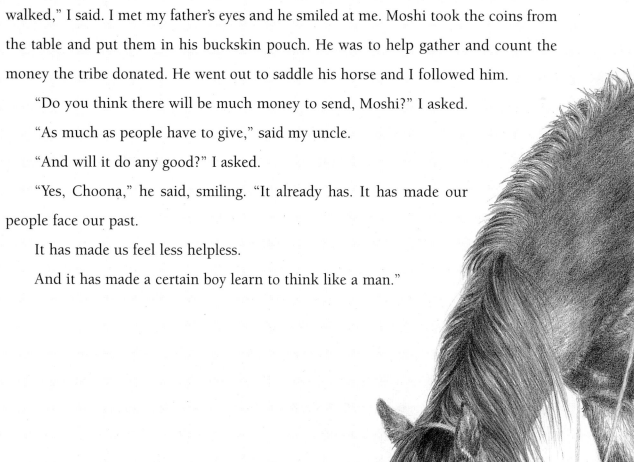

I can hear my uncle's voice. I can see him smile. I am an old man now, but I remember it all. No one has called me Choona in many, many years. I wear white man's clothes. Some of my grandchildren's children do not speak Choctaw. Our great traditions seem fragile now. But that day as I watched Moshi ride away on his horse, I felt the eagle spirit race through my blood. I walked across the yard, and as I reached its edge, I began to run. I ran at the mountain. I ran and ran until I had no breath left. I raised my face to the sky and shouted—

"Chahta hapia hoke. Chahta hapia hoke."

We are Choctaw.

Published in Ireland and Britain in 1998 by
Wolfhound Press Ltd
68 Mountjoy Square
Dublin 1, Ireland
Tel: (353-1) 874-0354
Fax: (353-1) 872-0207

Published in the United States and Canada by Beyond Words Publishing, Inc.
20827 N.W. Cornell Road, Suite 500
Hillsboro, Oregon 97124-9808

British Library Cataloguing in Publication Data
A catalogue record for this book is available from the British Library.

ISBN 0-86327-644-X

10 9 8 7 6 5 4 3 2 1

For their help with this book, many thanks are due to Chief Greg E. Pyle and the offices of the Choctaw Nation of Oklahoma, Judy Allen of the Bishinik, and the staff at Arrowhead, for their hospitality; Lena Noah (Talihoyo), Emma Fisher, Aubra and Dayna Lee, Kim Hunter, Anne Kinsella, and the Trócaire Library, for help with research; Marshall Gettys, for all the information on Choctaw dress and lifeways; the people who allowed me to photograph and draw them as potential models for the characters in this book, especially Quanah WhiteDeer (Choona) and his sisters and brothers Jincee, Rachel, Jesse, and Nashoba; Ronald EagleRoad, Eileen Burke, the McAlester Choctaw Community, and the Choctaw and Chickasaw people at the Kulli Homa dance grounds; the Irish Arts Council, Arts Flight, and the people of the Tyrone Guthrie Centre; Robert Dunbar; Ger Minogue, for word processing; Peter Malone, for the rescue work when things fell apart and the editorial work prior to that—thanks a million; Sarah WhiteDeer, for all the driving and good company in Oklahoma; and Don Mullan (European Director, CAIT), for helping me get started, encouraging me, and occasionally pushing me to get on with it! Biggest thanks of all to Gary WhiteDeer, without whom this book could not have been completed. Thanks, Gary, for your time, knowledge, and unfailing interest, for the many suggestions, corrections, and instruction in Choctaw ways and words, and in particular for the legend of Talihoyo and the image of the arrow shot through time. And lastly, to my family and friends, for all their support and tolerance!

Choctaw editor: Gary WhiteDeer
Irish editor: Peter Malone
U.S. editor: Michelle Roehm
Designer: Jane Aukshunas
Printed in Canada

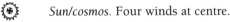

Author's Notes

The Choctaw Nation: Originally a large population of hunters and farmers who lived in the Southeastern region of the U.S. (Mississippi, Alabama, Louisiana), the Choctaw fought de Soto and the Spanish in 1540, and it was 150 years before other Europeans appropriated their lands. In 1786, the United States government recognised the sovereignty of the Choctaw as an independent nation. Along with the Creek, Cherokee, Seminole, and Chickasaw, they were sometimes known as the "Five Civilized Tribes." But all five "civilized tribes" were still forced off their land in the 1830s. The journey west to "Indian Territory" caused much death and suffering for these nations. Indian Territory, in turn, came under pressure from white settlers and eventually became the state of Oklahoma. Today there are 8,000 Choctaw in Mississippi, descendants of those who would not leave in 1831. Both Oklahoma and Mississippi Choctaw have their own constitutions, elect tribal councils and chiefs, and administer their own affairs.

The Irish Potato Famine (1845–1849): At this time, Ireland was governed by Britain. The majority of its eight million people lived on small patches of land rented from wealthy landlords. The potato is a nourishing vegetable that yields well even in poor soil, so the Irish had come to depend on it as their main food. A potato blight hit Europe in 1845 and destroyed most of that year's crop. In 1846 and 1847, there was a total crop failure. 1847 is known to the Irish as "Black '47". Over one million people died of starvation and famine-related diseases during these four years. Over one million people emigrated to other countries.

New Lands/Indian Territory: Lands to which the Southeastern tribes and others were removed between 1831 and 1839. In 1907, in violation of treaty agreements, this area became the state of Oklahoma. *Okla Homa* is Choctaw for "Red People".

Memphis Committee: A regional committee of the Society of Friends (Quakers). The Skullyville meeting with the tribal leaders was held on 23 March 1847. Just prior to this, on 9 February 1847, a huge public meeting was held in Washington D.C. under the chairmanship of the vice-president of the United States. The meeting discussed the Irish Potato Famine and "recommended that meetings should be held in every city, town and village so that a large national contribution might be raised" (Cecil Woodham-Smith, *The Great Hunger*).

Choctaw names and words used in *The Long March*:
Moshi: The name given to a mother's eldest brother. This uncle had a special relationship with, and responsibility for, his sisters' sons.
Talowa: "Song"
Hoshonti: "Cloud"
Talihoyo: "Rockwoman." The story of Talihoyo is a Choctaw legend.
Mishima Abi: "Over there he killed."
Nanih Waiyha: "Productive mountain." The Choctaw creation mound in Winston County, Mississippi.
Hapokani: "Grandmother"
Chahta hapia hoke: "We are Choctaw."

Choctaw symbols used in *The Long March*:

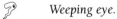 *River.* The Choctaw are on one bank and other peoples are on the opposite. Just as you can't stand on both sides of a river, you can't be of both cultures. But sometimes the banks come close together and touch.

 Sun/cosmos. Four winds at centre.

Weeping eye.

 *Death.*

Walking in circles.

 Sun/cosmos. Four corners at centre.

 Four corners of the Earth.

 Hand. Four corners at centre.